*Auntie Seagull's*

# Seafood Basics......

## buying . storing
## cleaning . cooking

## fish and shellfish

*by Julie V. Watson*

*Seacroft*

Copyright © 2010 Julie V Watson
First edition
First Printing

Cover Design & Production Facilitator: Pollywog Desktop Designs
Layout & Design: Seacroft
Author: Julie V. Watson

Published by:
Seacroft
P.O.Box 1204
Charlottetown
Price Edward Island
Canada C1A 7M8
www.seacroftpei.com

---

Library and Archives Canada Cataloguing in Publication

Watson, Julie V., 1943-
Auntie Seagull's Seafood Basics......buying . storing . cleaning
 . cooking fish and shellfish

Includes index.
ISBN 978-0-9687092-9-0

Shellfish, Fish, Species Information and Handling Guide, Atlantic
Canada.

# TABLE OF CONTENTS

# INTRODUCTION

The following pages provide basic how-to information about buying, storing, cleaning and preparing fish and shellfish that are common to Eastern North America and found in seafood markets every where. This information can be used in recipes of your choice.

With the growing interest in knowing where our food comes from, and a determination to support local harvesters, people are rediscovering the bounty that is around them. It is our feeling that our grandmothers, mothers, aunts and fishers have a huge pool of information gained through experience.  We drew upon them for the content of this book.

As a society we need to take control of what we consume and getting back to basics is the way to do it.  Over processed food is costly and contains ingredients we don't need. The convenience of boxed frozen products cannot be denied.  Neither can the benefits in both nutrition and flavour of fresh-from-the-sea choices.  Our recommendation is to save those costly processed items for true emergency meals, and to regain the joy of cooking from scratch as often as you can.

As author and designer we put this book together, but,  acknowledge that it is the wisdom of those who have been our teachers and mentors that make this information invaluable for the home cook.  We created Auntie Seagull to be their voice. Who is Auntie Seagull?   She represents many individuals met both as part of our own lives and as we explore topics of interest.  Auntie is a wise old bird. Her eyes aren't what they used to be, and her seashell jewelery might seem tacky to some, but she has seagull smarts and seagull wit.

Auntie remembers how to prepare food from scratch.  She knows how to make nourishing, and satisfying, meals with basic ingredients.  Most importantly she likes to share her knowledge and hopes that everyone learns the joy of serving up their best efforts without breaking the bank, slaving for hours, or relying on foods that have traveled for thousands of miles to get to our kitchens. Auntie believes in the locavor concept. She's been a neat chick since she hatched!!  Enjoy!

*Julie & Helen*

# Fish

## Fresh Fish

Although catching your own fish is the ideal way to guarantee freshness we obviously cannot do that each time we want it for dinner. Whether you are buying your fish from a fisherman or from your local store, be sure to check it for freshness by looking for the following:

* mild, fresh characteristic odour
* bright, full, clear eyes
* bright red gills
* bright characteristic sheen on scales
* tightly adhering scales
* firm or rigid body
* firm elastic flesh that does not retain imprint of fingers when handled

Fresh fillets and steaks:
* firm elastic flesh that does not separate from the bones
* fresh cut appearance, a moist and shiny appearance, no dry edges

**TERMINOLOGY**  (for the purpose of this book)
* Whole or round: just taken from the water - allow 1 lb per serving.
* Dressed or drawn: viscera removed - allow 1 pound per serving.
* Pan dressed: scaled, eviscerated, and usually with head, tail, and fins removed - allow 1 pound for 2 servings.
* Steaks: cross section slices - allow 1 pound for 2-3 servings.
* Fillets: meaty sides of fish cut lengthwise from the backbone - allow 1 pound for 3-4 servings.

## CLEANING FISH

There are only two unpleasant tasks connected with fishing - putting worms on hooks and cleaning your catch. To be perfectly frank, I have never cleaned a fish and I don't intend to. So, for the sake of making this book complete, I turned to experts to give you these instructions.

Cleaning means to eviscerate or gut, remove internal organs, head (if you desire), fins, and then to wash. There are two pieces of equipment essential for cleaning fish: a sharp knife, preferably with a thin blade, and lots of newspaper. Scissors can also be useful.

## TO CLEAN

* Using a sharp knife, slit the fish's belly from vent (anal opening) to gills. Remove the viscera (internal organs). Run the tip of the knife against the underside of back bone to remove the blood line. Wash fish under running water - rub lightly inside removimg remaining blood or unwanted material
* Next, remove the pelvic and pectoral fins by cutting the flesh along both sides of the fins. Pull the fin quickly toward the head to remove the root bones. Be careful not to tear the skin. The tail can be removed by cutting it off with a knife or scissors. (Removing fins and tail is a matter of choice; they can be left on, especially for serving a whole fish.)
* If you wish to remove the head, cut across the base of the gills, carefully taking the pectoral fins off as well. Now you have to sever the back bone. The best way to do this is to snap it by bending the head down over the edge of the table with one hand until it snaps while holding the fish firmly with the other hand. Should it be a big fish or a particularly hard backbone, enlist the help of your scissors or sharp knife to break the backbone.
* Be sure to cut rather than tear any flesh remaining between head and body.

## ROE

Any roe found when cleaning fish can be cooked and served with the fish or as an appetizer. Roe is found in the reproductive system of the fish. Soft roe, or sperm, is the substance found in the male fish. Hard roe is a mass or sac of fish eggs found in the female. Cod and herring roe are especially enjoyable. Cod roe is often smoked and makes an excellent pate or sandwich filling.

## SCALING

Scaling can be a messy job. Try to do it outside with a hose. The method is the same for indoors or out. Place the fish on a flat surface, holding it firmly with one hand. Using a sharp knife without a serrated edge, scrape towards the head, starting right at the tail. Take off all the scales, making sure you get those around the fins and up by the head. Rinse your fish and it's ready to clean. Wet fish are easier to scale, so if yours is not fresh out of the water soak it in cold water for a minute or two before you start. Wear old clothes and when finished clean the site and work area thoroughly hosing down if you are working outside - scales stick forever.

*Auntie says:*

*Your own fish scaler can be made by nailing 3 bottle caps, serrated edges up side by side on the end of a piece of wood. Rubbing the fish with vinegar loosens the scales.*

## FILLETING

Filleting is removing the flesh of the fish from the bones. Fillets can be skinned or not, according to your taste and planned use for the fish. If you do plan to leave the skin on, scale it before you fillet.

* With a sharp knife cut along the backbone line of the fish from tail to head. Next cut through skin and flesh right down beside the backbone to the ribs. Then cut the head off behind the gills.

* Holding the knife flat, cut the flesh down one whole side. Start at the head end, slicing it away from the ribs and backbone. Lift the flesh off in one piece.

* Turn the fish over and repeat the process on the other side.

* To skin the fillet, place the fillet skin side down, holding the tail firmly with one hand. Cut the skin from the flesh with quick, short strokes. Keep the knife blade close against and level with the skin so that no flesh is wasted. With a little practice you will be able to do this in one stroke, sliding the knife through and separating flesh from skin.

# Frozen Fish

Frozen fish can be purchased in fillets, whole, or in steaks. Look for:
* solidly frozen packages with no signs of drying out, freezer burn or discolouration. (Freezer burn is indicated by parched white areas.)
* no sign of frost or ice crystals when the package is opened.
* purchase packages stored below the load line of freezer cabinets.

Frozen fish need not be thawed before cooking. Measure the thickness of the fillet (a 1 lb package of frozen fish generally measures 1 inch) and allow 20 minutes of cooking time per inch for frozen or 15 minutes if partially thawed. Bake at 450 degrees F. To  sauté frozen cod, haddock, sole, flounder, or ocean perch, thaw slightly and cook over low to medium heat until done. To broil a frozen fillet block it is best to allow it to partially thaw, otherwise the surface becomes overcooked and the inside stays raw. Baste frequently.

**FREEZING YOUR OWN FISH**
So you went out fishing and came home with more than you can eat at one meal! It is not difficult to freeze fish. In fact, it is easier than blanching vegetables. Taking a few precautions first will help insure that the quality and flavour of the fish is saved.
* Freeze only fresh, cleaned and scaled fish (refer to cleaning and scaling instructions).
* After cleaning you can leave your fish whole, or cut into fillets or steaks.
* Freeze your fish quickly. Turn the temperature control to very cold well ahead of freezing time. Foods frozen fast have a finer texture than foods frozen slowly.
* Large fish may be placed on a wax-paper lined tray in the coldest part of your freezer. When solid, dip in ice-cold water and freeze again. Repeat until fish is coated with a glaze of ice, then put into freezer bags.

* If you are freezing fish fillets, separate with sheets of wax-paper, or freeze individually on a cookie sheet which has been lightly greased. They can then be packaged in one freezer bag and removed as you need them.
* Lean species can be dipped in a salt solution (1 cup salt per gallon of water) for 20 seconds in order to firm the flesh.
* Small fish can be frozen in a salt water solution. Make certain that the fish are completely covered with water. (I use strong plastic freezer bags or recycle milk bags. They do not split.) Remember to leave room for expansion as the water freezes. Place the plastic bag inside a bowl or a cardboard milk carton with the top cut off to keep the bag upright. Fill it with the fish, cover with water, and when it becomes a solid block remove the carton and seal.
* All frozen fish should be labeled with the date and contents. Use fatty species such as salmon, mackerel and trout within 2 months and lean species such as cod, haddock, perch, or smelt within 6 months.
* Don't forget to adjust your freezer to its most economical temperature after fish is frozen solid.
* If fish thaws, do not refreeze. Use immediately. Refreezing creates large ice crystals which break down cell walls, and causes loss of nutrition, flavour and texture.



*Before buying seafood from your local grocery store find out where it comes from. Frozen or packaged fish must show where it is from. Don't be fooled by "where it is packed". At the seafood counter the law says they must tell you where seafood originates. Demand to know. The majority of fish in many stores comes from South America, China, or other countries on the other side of the globe. It is our recommendation that you always strive to eat local foods. Both for freshness and adherance to our regulations, but also to keep your dollars at home.*

# Cooking Fish

'Fish is cooked to develop flavour, not to make it tender.' These words were written by well-known cooking expert James Beard, and I have never forgotten them. The most important rule of cooking fish is DO NOT OVERCOOK. No matter which method of cooking you choose, the rule always applies.


* Fish is cooked when the flesh flakes easily when parted with a fork, is opaque and milky in appearance, and slightly springy to the touch.
* Try to chose similar sized fish to cook together.
* Allow 1 lb of whole, small fish per serving and  ½ - ¾ lb if cleaned.


**BROILING**

Broiling, or cooking in your oven directly under a heat source, works well for fish and is not as messy a business as broiling steaks or chops. Most fish - whole, fillets, steaks, or chunks - can be broiled. Take care as the intense dry heat will easily overcook or dry the fish. It is best to broil fish that is over one inch thick. Thinner fish will end up looking and tasting like a piece of leather if you are not careful.
* Remember to leave the oven door slightly open when broiling.
* Preheat the oven to broil at 550 degrees F for 5-10 minutes.
* Oil or grease a shallow pan so that the fish does not stick. (For quick cleanup, line a pan with well-greased foil.)
* Lightly dust fish with flour. Shaking fish gently in a paper bag with a small amount of flour is a good method. Seasonings are best added after cooking.
* Set the fish on the pan. If the skin is left on fillets, put the skin side down.
* Dot the top well with butter or oil. All but the most fatty fish (such as mackerel) will need basting.
* Place fish 3-4 inches from the heat source, usually the top rack in your oven. Delicate white fish should be moved a bit further away. If using lemon juice or sauces, move the rack further from the heat, about 5-6 inches.
* Cooking time depends on the thickness of your fish. Measure the thickest part from the top of the fish, including the stuffing. For every 1 inch of fish, cook 10 minutes.

*  Fillets will take 5-8 minutes to broil depending on the thickness and should not need moistening. Check after 4 minutes to make certain they are not drying at the edges.

*  Steaks take from 6-10 minutes, again depending on the thickness. Turn once during cooking after about 3 minutes. Baste to begin, after turning, and again if needed.

*  Certain whole fish broil nicely when split and spread open with the skin side down. Try leaving the head on - it will be juicier. I usually allow 3-4 minutes on one side before turning, then baste or oil the fish and cook for a further 6-8 minutes. Baste according to the variety of fish. Baste the thinner edges more frequently. There is no real rule for length of time this fish takes to cook. Judge it by testing the thickest part for doneness.

## BAKING

*  Preheat oven to 450 degrees F.

*  Brush fresh or frozen fish with oil or butter or substitute tomato juice if you are diet conscious.

*  Place in a greased casserole. Season with salt and pepper and bake in the centre of the oven for the necessary cooking time. Normally when baking fish, the directions for cooking are included in the recipe.

## STUFFING FISH

Most larger fish can be stuffed and baked, or cooked on the barbecue.

*  Clean the fish, then wash and dry.

*  Sprinkle the inside of the fish with a little salt.

*  Put stuffing in the fish loosely, allowing about ¾ cup for each pound of fish. (Slightly more will be needed if you have removed the back-bone.)

*  The opening can be closed with toothpicks, small skewers, or can be sewn with string or heavy thread.

*  The stuffed fish should be cooked on a greased baking dish and brushed with oil, or wrapped in buttered aluminum foil.

*  Bake at 450 degrees F, allowing 10 minutes for each inch of thickness of the fish measured at the thickest part, including the stuffing.

## STEAMING

Steaming is an excellent way of cooking fish, especially when it is to be served with a sauce. It is very good for people who must restrict fat in their diets.

You need a cooking utensil which allows the fish to cook without it coming into contact with the liquid. There are metal steamers and bamboo steamers which fit into a wok or over a frying pan, or improvise a steamer by laying several bamboo sticks across a wok and setting the fish on them, or set a plate on small cans with holes pierced in their sides, inside a sauce pan with a cover.

Be sure to grease a metal steamer pan where it will be in contact with the fish to prevent sticking. Never grease a bamboo steamer as the bamboo will absorb the oil or fat and not be useful for vegetables. Instead lay the fish on a bed of lettuce leaves to prevent sticking.

Any cut of fish can be steamed. I prefer to steam larger whole fish or fillets. Fatty fish are best cooked in a way that takes some of the fat from the flesh, such as broiling or pan frying.

* For **stove-top steaming** use water or fish stock. The water can have wine or vinegar added, or be seasoned with a sprinkling of herbs. My favorite combination is to use half water, half white wine and just a pinch of tarragon.
* Cooking time will depend on the amount and thickness of fish. 10 minutes should do for 12 pounds of fish. Fish should flake easily when cooked.
* Any liquid left can be used to prepare a sauce or for stock.

* When **oven steaming** the flavour and juices are sealed in and the fish steams in its own liquid. Foil works best for this method.
* Preheat the oven to 450 degrees F.
* Place fish on a piece of well-greased foil big enough to wrap the fish tightly or, if preferred place fish on well-greased parchment, wrap, then seal in foil.
* Season fish with salt and pepper.
* Measure it at the thickest part.
* Wrap the fish tightly in the foil, making double folds, pinching to make them airtight.
* Place on a baking sheet or shallow pan and bake. Allow 10 minutes cooking time per inch thickness for fresh fish and 20 minutes per 1 inch for frozen fish. Allow at least an extra 5 minutes for fresh and 10 minutes for frozen fish to allow for heat to penetrate the foil and fish.

## POACHING

Poaching puts the fish right in the liquid to cook. It can be done either on the stove top or in the oven. Almost any fish can be cooked with this method although lean, white, whole fish or fillets are best. Smoked fish poaches especially well.

Poached fish tends to fall apart. If you wish to keep it intact it is best to wrap it to keep it together. **Cheesecloth** works well. Wrap fish in cheesecloth tying both ends to use as handles. Cheesecloth is easier to handle if you wet it in the liquid before wrapping the fish. When the fish is done, carefully lift out and place on a platter. Open the cheesecloth by slitting with a sharp knife or scissors. Using a knife, carefully remove the skin from the fish. When one side is done, use the cheesecloth to turn the fish (removing it at the same time) then skin the other side. **Parchment paper** can also be used for wrapping fish. This method of cooking is making a comeback with the growing popularity of oriental cooking. Parchment paper is available in gourmet shops, but years ago it was used commercially for wrapping foods such as butter, and saved and reused by the cook.

* Dampen the fish, then place on dampened parchment paper. Sprinkle fish with salt and measure at thickest point. Add a tablespoon each of chopped onion and celery, then wrap securely by drawing up the corners and tying with string or a metal twist tie.

* Fish can be poached in a variety of liquids - water, milk or wine with seasonings. One of the more popular liquids is Court Bouillon. Fish should simmer rather than boil.

* Use a wide shallow pan, large enough to hold the fish. On the stove top a frying pan with a lid does nicely. When preparing larger quantities of fish in the oven, use a roasting pan with a lid.

* Use enough liquid to just cover the fish. Add a dab of butter and bring

to a boil before placing fish in liquid. Cover and simmer. Allow 10-15 minutes cooking time for 2 lbs of fish, or 1 inch of thickness. Use the standard test for doneness.

* Remove the fish from the liquid carefully.
* Never throw away the liquid used to poach fish. It is excellent for sauces and chowders. If you can't use it right away, freeze it.

## BOILING

Boiling fish is a common method of cooking here in Atlantic Canada, particularly for mackerel and salt cod. Boiling is similar to poaching, but always uses water, to which a small amount of vinegar can be added.

## PAN FRYING

Pan frying is probably the most common method of cooking fish. Whether you use butter, margarine or cooking oil is a matter of personal preference.

* Season each portion - fish can be whole, fillets, steaks, or frozen portions and should be pan ready. Cover lightly with flour. Dip in liquid (milk or beaten egg), coat with flour or crumbs again. (Gently shake in a plastic bag or use a bowl.)
* Heat ½ inch of oil or butter in a skillet. Fry on both sides over medium heat. Drain on a paper towel and serve immediately.

*Antie says:*

*Cooks love to have left over fish. Bones and skin removed, it is perfect in sandwiches when mixed with a little mayo, chopped celery or onion and even grated carrots. Or mix left over fish and mashed potatoes with an egg and seasonings. Form into fish cakes and fry in a hot pan until browned.*

## SAUTEING

Small, whole fish are best for sauteing (frying quickly in a little fat), rather than larger fish, fillets or steaks which are likely to stick to the pan. Trout, smelt and capelin are particularly good.
* Dip the cleaned fish in milk and roll in flour.

* Have butter or oil in a frying pan - enough to cover the bottom of the pan. When it is hot (be careful not to burn it), add the fish and saute on one side until brown, then carefully turn and brown the other side. (Using half olive oil, then adding butter helps prevent the butter from burning.)



*For an easy snack fry up some sardines, or small fish like smelt. An old recipe says dry on blotting paper, you can use paper towels! Dip in lemon juice, roll in breadcrumbs and fry in butter until a nice brown. Serve on toast.*

## DEEP FRYING

Although fish and chips are one of the most popular ways of eating fish, successful deep frying is no simple task.  Nor, is it an exceptionally difficult one.  You just have to go about it the right way!

* Heat the fat in a deep fryer (or a heavy pot with deep sides), to 375 degrees F.  To test for correct temperature, a 1 inch cube of bread should brown in 60 seconds. It is best to save fat from frying fish and use only for that purpose.
* There are two ways to prepare the fish. Use a batter or dip the fish in beaten egg and roll in flour, cornmeal or breadcrumbs. Give fish a gentle shake to get rid of loose coating.
* Place your fish in a wire frying basket and lower into the fat or gently slide it in, taking care not to splash. Separate the pieces with a fork if necessary. Cook 3-5 minutes - fish will float to the top when cooked. Remove with a strainer or by lifting the basket and removing with tongs.
* Make certain that the fat returns to a high cooking temperature before starting your second batch.
* Be very careful when deep frying foods. Spattering fat can cause burns and fires. Keep a box of baking soda handy to put out any flames. If a fire occurs put cover over pot and turn off the heat.
* Certain fish takes better to deep frying than others. Basically, any white fish can be used. Fatty fish are better cooked other ways.

# Fish Species
## Mackerel

Sleek, silvery mackerel were my first taste of Prince Edward Island seafood.  One summer we joined a fishing charter out of North Rustico. Not satisfied with hand-held jig lines, my family had taken along fishing rods only to find they were of little use. They were too cumbersome and inclined to get tangled. Soon all reverted to using the time-honoured tradition of jigging. Fate was smiling on us that day as we pulled in fish after fish, waiting only long enough for crew members to take them off our hooks and re-bait.

Frying these mackerel over a campfire, in our old cast iron pan, addicted me for life. Even today after sampling hundreds of fish dishes, nothing tastes as good as mackerel, pan fried or baked or grilled, split with skin side down on the barbecue. I often think that this memory had a lot to do with us giving up our lifestyle in Ontario and making our home on the Island.

Atlantic mackerel are easily distinguished by the dark tiger-like stripings on the back, the blue and silver body, and the small finlets near the tail. Related to the tuna, it has the same sleek look.

Mackerel is a nourishing and fatty fish. It has a fine strongish flavour - best when absolutely fresh. In fact they are never quite as good as when right out of the sea and into the pot.

*Antie says:*

*Consider the simple way a fisherman cooks mackerel on the boat for his own lunch. In a pot of seawater put potatoes cut into chunks, quartered onions and mackerel that have been cleaned, with heads and tails removed. Bring to a boil and simmer until potatoes are tender and skin begins to come loose from the mackerel.*

Fresh mackerel does not keep as well as other fish that have less oil in their tissues. Thus, salted, pickled and smoked mackerel have been used since the days of the pioneers.

On a commercial fishing basis, mackerel ranks in importance with other fish harvested in local waters. Prior to 1870 most of the mackerel was caught by hook and line from boats. They bite greedily on almost any bait, especially if it moves. Mackerel travel in schools, so are an attractive fish to pursue. Fishermen would lure schools by throwing bait, usually ground up fish, into the water. While this method was gradually given up on a commercial basis, it is still used for sport fishing during the summer.

Commercial fishermen turned to seines, nets, weirs and trawls, especially during the times when Russian trawlers came in close to shore to buy mackerel.

Catches increased over the years, making mackerel very economical. It became readily available canned, salted, smoked and frozen, and became a popular replacement for the then more expensive canned salmon or tuna.

One of the nicest things about mackerel is the fact that you do not have to scale them. While it is a fallacy that they have no scales, the scales are certainly not troublesome.

# Tuna

Atlantic Canada  is known world wide for its bluefin tuna sports fishing. Enthusiasts come from near and far to try and hook one of the big fish, making charter boats an important part of the fishing economy.

This large fish visits our waters during the summer and fall of each year. A tuna is beautifully streamlined with a bluntly pointed nose and a robust body that tapers evenly from the shoulder to a long, slim tail. The head has tightly closing jaws, flat gill-covers and eyes set flush with the surrounding surface.

The body is completely covered with scales, including a corselet of large scales in the shoulder region. Some of the fins fold into grooves or depressions thus giving a smooth contour to the body. With such a shape it is not surprising that bluefin are among the swiftest and widest ranging fishes in the sea.

Adult bluefins are metallic blue with a greenish sheen on the back, shading through silver on the sides to white on the belly. In contrast, young bluefin have conspicuous white vertical bars and spots along the sides which disappear gradually as the fish grow.

In Canada bluefin are caught primarily by rod and reel, although some hooks can now be set from buoys by fishermen only interested in the catch and not the sport.

If the sports fishermen is fortunate enough to hook one of these big fish, it normally remains the property of the boat owner. The sale of the catch can be a  very important part of the fishermen's income.

Government regulations prohibit the consumption of this tuna in Canada because of the mercury content which is just slightly above the level allowed.  Instead, bluefin tuna is air freighted to Japan. They are packed in ice for shipment, rarely frozen, and sold as fresh fish. Tuna is a delicacy for the Japanese and is usually eaten raw.

Those wishing to fish bluefin tuna for the sport can do so from several ports in the region during government regulated fishing seasons.

Of course today we consumers enjoy tuna from the can.  In fact when times are lean it can be a staple for casseroles, and we all enjoy tuna salad sandwiches from time to time.

*Antie says:*

*If a fish is fresh its eyes will be slightly protruding, bright and clear. If they are pink, sunken, or cloudy the fish is stale. If the gills are gray turn away. They should be red or pink.*

# Smelt

Smelt, along with eels, are particularly appreciated by fishermen because they can be readily caught at a time when ice on the water prevents most other kinds of fishing.

Smelts have long been fished through holes cut in the ice of estuaries. It is easy enough to tell where the smelt enter rivers for spawning by the number of ice fishing shacks dotting the ice.

When arriving at his shack, the fisherman must first open up the fishing hole. That may be a job for an axe if it is very cold, or at least a need to clean out any ice crystals which have formed on the water during his absence.  This is done with an ordinary household sieve. Then bait is thrown in to attract smelt under the hole and the fisherman's expertise with the spear comes into play. It takes a sure eye and swift dexterity to spear the swift little fish.

Some smelt fishing in the Maritimes is also carried out by trapping smelt in box nets or bag nets set either in open water, or through the ice. A small amount of fishing takes place in the fall, and during spring runs in creeks and rivers..

Smelt are a small, slender, silvery fish - olive green along the back. They rarely exceed 9 inches in length. The American Smelt, as it is properly known, is often confused with the similar, but unrelated, silverside or capelin, which is a close relative.
* These delicate little fish are not cleaned in the same way as larger fish. Cut off the head just behind the gills, pulling the insides through the gills as you do so. If this proves difficult, use a teaspoon to scoop the insides out. If desired, cut off the tail and fins with scissors.
* At certain times in their life cycle smelts need to have scales removed. This is best done by holding them under a running tap and rubbing against the lie of the scales with your fingers or a brush.
* Smelt take well to freezing, and it is very simple to do. Cut and wash them, then package in plastic bags or tightly-folded freezer wrap. Be sure they are sealed properly and freeze quickly. If using a plastic bag it is best to draw the air from the bag by sucking it out through a straw before sealing.

**CAPELIN**

Small fish closely related to smelt, Capelin are found in the Gulf of St. Lawrence and often hooked by fishermen in estuaries or from wharves.

They are slender fish, a translucent olive-green on the back, shading to silver on the sides and white over the belly. At maturity they range from 5-8 inches in length.

Capelin are fished commercially in some areas.  Although used mainly for bait, fertilizer and dog food in the early part of this century, they are becoming increasingly in demand for human consumption in their fresh, frozen and canned state, particularly in Central Europe.


**SILVERSIDES**

A small silvery fish, sometimes confused with smelts. They are fished in the fall and many fishermen refer to them as capelin, although they are different.

Capelin and silversides can be treated just as smelt.

# Trout

Trout are held in high esteem for their delicious flavour and for their appearance. They are appearing more frequently on tables as trout farming becomes more popular and successful.

There are several types of trout farming operations: fish kept in ponds usually fed by fresh water springs, in tanks, and larger trout raised in seawater pens in bays and inlets on the coast. Rainbow and sea trout are among the favourites raised this way and can often be obtained fresh at farmers' markets.

For sports fishermen, brook and rainbow trout are a favourite, angled in streams, rivers and estuaries. Brook trout are the most popular and plentiful of inland fish. Bait, flies and lures are used to catch these fish which range from ¼ pound up to 4 pounds in weight.

The number of rainbow trout has decreased, although they are considered the ultimate catch. This changes as streams are stocked  through aquaculture projects. Rainbow trout can be identified by their metallic blue back, speckled with black spots.

Larger trout, commonly called sea trout, can be caught in estuaries and the sea.

The best time of year for lake angling is from mid-April to mid-June, then again from late August through September.  You need a fishing license.

Should you be out in the woods fishing, remember that trout should be kept clean, dry, and cool. If you don't happen to have ice and a cooler along, remember the tricks of our forefathers. Wrap the fish in moss and keep it out of the sun.

*Antie says:*

*There is nothing quite as good as bacon wrapped trout cooked in the great outdoors. Bacon will keep the flesh from burning and gives it a wonderful flavor, especially if you use smoked bacon. All you need is a cleaned trout, bacon, a lemon, lemon pepper and maybe a sprinkle of salt.*

*Rub the outside of the trout with lemon. Squeeze the remaining juice into the cavity and sprinkle with lemon pepper and salt if desired. Wrap the trout with bacon slices to cover. You may find it easier to use skewers or toothpicks to secure the bacon. Place fish on grill, and cook for 4-10 minutes depending on thickness of fish. Only turn once in cooking as bacon may become brittle.*

# Atlantic Salmon

My first experience with Atlantic salmon occurred when we were driving past the West River bridge in Bonshaw, PEI.  Glancing over towards the river to see if many fishermen were about, we saw one carrying a monstrous fish, so large he had it draped over his arms with the head hanging down on one side and the tail flopping on the other side. Never having seen a fish of this size, I sat with my mouth hanging open - to discover later it was an Atlantic salmon.

Each spring, hopeful anglers using unweighted flies try to hook one of the returning salmon. There is a certain romance attached to the salmon for its spectacular ability to leap falls, proceed up rapids and fish ladders, following its ancient mating instinct.

At one time wild salmon were a staple and important food item but now they are a luxury. Demand is in danger of stripping the supply. Restocking projects are helping to ensure the future of this and other important fish.  Farm raised salmon has become a household staple, and wild a rare occurrence.

Identification of salmon can be tricky. At certain stages in their development they resemble Brook (speckled) trout. The main differences are: the trout has a squarer tail than the salmon's forked one, the dorsal fin of a salmon has no dark bars or patches - as does the trout - and there are no black spots on the body or cheeks of the trout.
*  Atlantic salmon have a stout but streamlined body, small scales and a small fleshy fin on the back just in front of the tail. Colour varies with age and stage of development, but when in the sea they are silvery on the sides and belly. The back varies through shades of brown, green and blue. There are numerous black spots, usually x-shaped, scattered along the body.
*  When caught fresh, the cheeks and roe are special delicacies. Cheeks should be lightly floured and pan fried in a mixture of half oil and half butter. Roe can be sautéed or poached. When fresh salmon has been kept for a few days it loses the creamy curd from between the flakes.
* A very old cookbook advises that salmon require longer cooking than other fish, and should not be undercooked. Tastes have changed today, however, and overcooked fish is felt to be dry.  Wise cooks find their own level of doneness.

# Herring

In days gone by, herring was often referred to as the poor man's friend - abundant, nutritional and delicious. Unfortunately, today they are not eaten as much as they should be. Their flesh is tender and delicate, although boney. Herring was very important when the family had to preserve as much food as possible for the long winter months. Herring was dried, salted, kippered, soused (pickled), and smoked. Kippers, long associated with the Scottish, are herring which are salted and dried or smoked. You may occasionally see a reference to bloaters. These are also herring, but the older fatter ones.

Herring usually enter the waters around Alantic Canada just after the off-shore ice breaks up, making them a welcome change after winter fare. Some herring is sold commercially. Herring is used by fishermen for bait to lure lobsters into the trap. Although it is quite possible to catch herring on a hook and line yourself, most  fishermen catch herring by setting gill nets near the shore.

In this section we also mention anchovies, sardines, shad, and alewife - all of which belong to the herring family. All except anchovies are found in the Gulf of St. Lawrence, although sardines are found infrequently. The few sardines caught are usually mistaken for smelt. Shad has been mostly fished out.

*Antie says:*
*Old-timers valued herring as a food even saying nothing could beat herring boiled with blue potatoes as a restorative after illness.*

## GASPEREAU

Gaspereau are members of the herring family. They are fairly well-known,  although most people don't fish them to eat, but rather to use as bait. There is usually a run of gaspereau coming into rivers to spawn in mid-May and lasting till the end of June. They arrive before other bait fish so are welcomed by fishermen. If you have some gaspereau, don't hesitate to try eating them, just treat them as herring.

**HERRING ROE**

* When cleaning herring save the roe. There are two kinds: soft herring roe, which is the sperm from the male, and hard herring roe which is the eggs from the female. These are also referred to as peas and melts (melts being the milt from the male). Roe must be used from herring within 1-2 hours after catching the fish, as it quickly spoils.

* Both soft and hard roe should be carefully separated from the fish, washed gently and patted dry. Roe can be coated in a little seasoned flour and sauteed for a few minutes in butter, or coated in egg and bread crumbs and fried in shallow or deep fat.

* Here is another excellent way of cooking soft herring roe that makes it easily digestible. Put the herring roe on a plate with butter, a little seasoning and cream or milk. Cover with a second plate and steam over a pan of rapidly boiling water for about 10 minutes. Serve on hot toast garnished with paprika, butter and chopped parsley. The cooked roe may be put into a white sauce or used instead of flaked fish in a fish pie.

* If you want to use either soft or hard roe as a pate, steam as above, but use very little milk because you want the roe a little drier. When cooked, pound until soft. Add seasoning, a squeeze of lemon and extra butter, if desired, to make it spread easier. I have also read that a little anchovy paste added to this is delicious. Don't use salt until you have tasted the mixture.

* Roe can also be broiled by putting into a broiler pan and brushing with melted butter.

# Kippers

A kipper is a herring which has been split, cleaned, washed, steeped in brine for a short time, then smoked over smoldering wood chips. The kipper is generally cooked and served plain, save for perhaps the addition of a pat of butter or a wedge of lemon. Kippers are usually packed in pairs. They are available with the heads on or off, in fresh and frozen form or in boil-in-bag packs. Allow 1 whole kipper or 2 small ones per serving.

One point about kippers to keep in mind is that, although mildly cured, they are almost as perishable as fresh, unprocessed fish. Keep them under refrigeration at all times, and don't keep them long.

When buying kippers, look for plumpness, firm flesh, glossy skin, and wholesome aroma.
* Kippers are cooked by grilling, baking in foil, boiling in a plastic bag, poaching, and jugging.
* Poaching and jugging give a moister, less salty kipper.
* Don't try to grill or fry canned kippers, they're too moist and will fall apart.
* Which ever method is used, the cooking time is short because, as a result of processing, kippers are already partially cooked.

# White Fish

Some of the best fishing grounds in the world are off the eastern seaboard of Canada. Not all of the fish mentioned here are landed frequently in my home province, Prince Edward Island, but they are certainly available. Cold waters produce a firm-textured, white-coloured fish with a light, delicate flavour. White fish includes cod, flounder, haddock, hake, sole, shark, swordfish, and turbot. They are considered 'lean' fish. Most white fish are interchangeable in  recipes. For basic cleaning and cooking instructions, see the fish section beginning on page 5.  Flat fish or flounder are covered in the following pages. When broiling, lean fish must be basted well and frequently as it will dry out faster than the fatty fishes.

**COD**

Cod is probably the best known of all the white fish. Today, as in the beginning of the fishery in the 16th century, the sovereignity of cod fish is unshaken among the groundfish species on the Atlantic coast.
* Cod, to many, seems to be lacking in flavour. This is not a disadvantage however, because it means that cod with its meaty texture is very adaptable.
* Atlantic Cod are classified as groundfish, that group of fish that live close to the ocean bottom. They have an average weight of 5 pounds and usually do not exceed 60 pounds. Cod older than 16 years are not common  these days; much younger fish make up the bulk of the commercial catches.

* Cod are capable of changing colour from grey to green to brown, to match their surroundings.
* Tom cod is not related to the cod. It is a smaller fish but is also a white fish caught in small numbers.

**Tongues, Cheeks, Sounds, Roe:** parts of the cod most revered by early Maritimers, are often neglected today. Tongues and cheeks are self explanatory. Sounds are the air bladder of the fish and the roe - the eggs. It is said that cod cheeks make an excellent substitute for scallops and can be cooked the same way.



*Should you be cleaning your own cod, don't throw tongues and cheeks away. They are delicious when pan fried in butter. Just one of the possibilities.*

## HADDOCK

Haddock are one of the most sought after fish. They are not commonly fished in the Gulf of St. Lawrence, although some are caught.
* Many Maritimers prefer haddock on their dinner plate to most other kinds of fish because of its firm, white flesh, which separates into meaty flakes.
* Haddock belongs to the same family as other ground fishes and is closely related to cod, pollock and hake. Freshly caught haddock are dark purple-grey on the head and back. Below the lateral line the colouration lightens to silver-grey with a slight pink cast.
* Haddock are not fished for sport. They are taken primarily by commercial vessels using otter trawls. The average size is about 10 pounds and 25" long. Because of declining stocks, fishing is carefully regulated.
* Split and smoked haddock are called Finnan Haddie.

## BOSTON BLUEFISH (POLLOCK)

The Boston bluefish, pollock, is a member of the cod family. For years, these spirited, saltwater fish were unappreciated except by sports fishermen. Now, they are eagerly sought as a replacement for the less abundant haddock.

* Like the haddock, they are found in the Atlantic from Labrador to Cape Cod. They are rarely caught in the Gulf of Saint Lawrence, although they do prefer the shallow coastal waters to ocean depths.
* This fish has a hearty flavour and a firm flake, making it especially popular as a commercially breaded product.


## HAKE (BASQUELLE)

Hake are said to be one of the under-utilized fish in the Canadian fisheries. They are harvested mostly by fishing fleets of other nations, with the quantities caught in Canada normally marketed whole, dressed or frozen.
* There are two kinds of hake familiar to Atlantic waters, white hake and silver hake. White hake are somewhat cod-like but have only two, rather than three, back fins, and only one belly fin. The colour varies considerably along the back, usually from reddish to muddy brown, and the belly is pale grey, yellowish or white. They are normally caught by trawlers, gillnets, longlines, and handlines. Silver hake are members of the cod family, but are more slender and have two back fins. They are dark grey with silver underparts. When freshly taken from the water, they are an iridescent silver, but the bright colour soon fades.
* Hake is a very delicate tasting fish.
* In 1982, the PEI Fisherman's Association decided to change the hake's name to Basquelle hoping that the new name would help the image and sales.


## FLATFISH/SOLE

Flounder, plaice, sole, brill, turbot, and skate are all flat fish and included in the flatfish family. They all have a very delicate flavour and texture.
* Basically, there are four important species of small flatfish found along Canada's east coast: American plaice, yellowtail, witch and winter flounder. The winter flounder caught in substantial numbers off PEI, is commonly known as the blackjack. These four are commercially marketed as 'sole' and collectively make up the most important Atlantic flatfish catch after cod.
* Although the four species differ somewhat in size, appearance, distribution, and abundance, they are similar in that their bodies are flat

and both eyes are on the same side of the head. Their underside is white, while their top side is pigmented, resembling the bottom over which they live and feed.



## HALIBUT

Atlantic halibut are giant members of the flatfish family and command the highest price of any flatfish.

* Halibut inhabit the Atlantic and the Gulf of St. Lawrence and are also farmed. They are readily distinguished from most other flatfish by their large mouth and forked tail. The upperside is greenish-brown to very dark brown with scattered blotches. The underside ranges from white in small fish, to grey or mottled grey-white. Halibut can become very large - over 100 pounds.

* They are caught with longlines and trawls and marketed fresh or frozen, usually in the form of steaks and fillets.

## TURBOT

Turbot is very similar to halibut, although a little fuller in flavour.

* They are yellowish or greyish-brown and, unlike other flatfish, the dark pigmentation is fairly uniform over the whole body, although the colouring is slightly lighter on the blind side. The tail, like that of halibut, is forked, but the lateral line is straight not arched.

* The areas where these fish are caught include the deep waters of the Gulf of St. Lawrence. Traditionally a line trawl fishery, gill nets are now also being used to harvest them.

* The bulk of the catch goes to market as fresh or frozen fillets.

## OCEAN PERCH

Full-flavoured ocean perch is a big retail selling species. You have probably eaten it in a restaurant, more than likely breaded and deep fried.

* Ocean perch, also known as redfish or rosefish, are relatively small, spiny fish with an orange to flame-red body which contrasts vividly with their large black eyes. The average weight is about 1 pound. Because perch grow very slowly, they are especially vulnerable to intensive fishing.
* Almost the entire catch is sold in frozen form as ocean perch fillets.

# Smoked, Salted and Dried Fish

Back in the days when families had no electricity they relied upon their own preservation methods. Dried fish was as important as pickled meats. All methods of preserving were utilized for fish, but the most common were salting, smoking and drying.

Exposing fish to smoke produces an appetizing flavour and temporarily preserves the fish. The best seafoods to smoke are those with a high fat content such as mackerel, salmon, oysters, eel, and herring. The fish must be smoked over certain varieties of wood, such as oak, maple or apple, in order to develop the proper flavour. Thanks to the presence of fine fish smoking operations, smoked fish is finding renewed popularity due to its wonderful flavour.
* Smoked fish should be cared for in the same manner as fresh fish. It may be stored in the refrigerator for 2-3 days or frozen for later use.
* Salt and dried fish keep indefinitely, as long as they are kept free of moisture. To freshen, cover with cold water for 12 hours. Change 2-3 times for salt fish. Drain, add fresh water and simmer until fish flakes easily (20-25 min).

# Eels

Our first eel was caught with rod and reel off the wharf at North Rustico, as was our second and third. Our immediate reaction was to get this horrid thing off our hooks even if we had to cut the line.

That first time, an elderly onlooker was more than pleased to remove the eel from our lines and even kindly offered to take the thing away for us. A little bit of asking around and we soon learned just how popular the eel is. Of course, most eels are not fished by our method. They are usually taken through the ice in winter with spears. Eels are found in estuaries and shallow creeks usually quite close to the sea.

## TO SKIN EELS

Eels, like fish which are slippery, are easier to handle if you rub some salt on your hands. The home of the devoted eel eater can often be identified by the nails where eels have been skinned. One woman up West is reported to have a line of nails in her windowsill in case a large catch comes. The secret is to skin it properly - that's where the nail comes into play.

* Slit the neck of the eel just below the head, from the underside. Leave the backbone uncut. Tie a string around the remaining flesh and fasten securely to the nail. Using a pair of pliers, pull the skin down and off the eel. The process is sort of like turning a glove inside out. When the skin is off, slit the stomach and clean the innards using a fork or knife. Wash your eel and then cut into 2 inch pieces. With your knife slit along the backbone (this stops the eel from jumping around in the hot pan - a rather unpleasant tendency they have). Remove any obvious fat for the best results when cooking.

*Auntie says:*

*To Cook Eels it is best to parboil the pieces for 2-3 minutes as eel flesh is oily. They can then be pan fried or used in a recipe of choice. They must be eaten while very fresh, so used to be often sold alive.*

# Shellfish

Shellfish are the most glamorous of all seafood. Atlantic Canadians are especially fortunate to have an abundance and variety of shellfish as easy to obtain as fish. While it is true that some shellfish, like lobster, scallops or oysters, are expensive enough to be a special treat or luxury item; others, like clams, mussels and quahogs, are very economical.

Shellfish are becoming increasingly important. As fish stocks are depleted and costs of catching and processing them continue to rise, rapid advances in the technology of farming shellfish are making them more accessible. Oysters, mussels and scallops are now successfully farmed and the future could see other shellfish farmed as well.

**NOTE:** There are rules and regulations governing the harvesting of certain kinds of shellfish and certain areas where taking shellfish is not recommended, due to unsafe waters caused by natural tidal blooms, run off from agricultural fields and even pollution. Check with the Department of Fisheries for these regulations.

**Never harvest shellfish without checking for both legal harvesting regulations and safety on a particular day.**

# Clams

Clam digging is an integral part of Maritime life. It is a full-or part-time activity for many individuals and is often used to supplement the income of inshore fishermen. Clams are also farmed. There are many varieties of clams - some burrow deep into the sand, like the soft-shelled clam and the razor clam, others, such as quahogs, live close to the surface. Clams are often sandy inside. To free them of sand, fill your bucket with fresh salt water and add a handful of oatmeal. Leave the clams for a few hours. They will digest the cereal and eliminate most of the sand.

*Antie says:*

*Gulls particularly love clams. They take them up into the air, and let them drop to crack open on the ground below. Then they swoop down to demolish their catch. Watch the pavement in areas such as Covehead Bridge or Panmure Beach and avoid these shells when driving. Many a tire has been changed after gulls have enjoyed clams for dinner.*

**SOFT-SHELLED CLAMS**
* Have a chalky white shell, and grow up to 4 inches long - although they are mature and tastiest at just over 2 inches in length.
* This species lives at the mid-tide mark, in sandy or muddy sediments, burrowing into the ground 5-8 inches. Recognize them by an oval-shaped hole in the sand. (To make sure it's a clam down there, stick your finger in the hole. If it goes down easily it's a clam.)
* The shells on these clams are very fragile. They can be dug with a shovel, but you may end up with many broken ones. Digging them with your hands or using a toilet plunger to uncover them will not break so many. These clams characteristically squirt when caught. They are a delicate and tender clam.

## HARD-SHELLED CLAMS

* The Indian word for hard-shelled clam is quahog; and locals often use the term. Small quahogs are often called cherrystone clams.
* Larger quahogs tend to be tough, so are often used minced in chowders. Their shell is thick, hard, and grayish-white and can grow up to 5 inches.
* Quahogs live at the low water mark and just beyond. They do not bury themselves very deep and can be caught by hand, fork, tongs, or rakes.

## BAR OR SURF CLAMS

One of the largest clams.
* They have thick, chalky shells covered with a shiny, yellow-to-brown skin or membrane.
* These clams are tough and best steamed and minced in chowders or stews.

*Antie says:*

*To Steam Clams scrub the shells until clean. Allow them to stand for 15-20 minutes in clean, salted water (1/3 cup salt to 1 gallon water). Place clams on a bed of seaweed (if you have it) in a large kettle which contains 1 inch of water. Or put them into a sieve or steamer. Cover tightly. Bring to a boil. Steam for 8-10 minutes until the shells open. Discard any shells that do not open.*

*Reserve broth to use in a chowder, or season and serve as a clam soup*

# Mussels

If there is a seafood that is 'up and coming' in Prince Edward Island, it's mussels. Once referred to by the Scottish as the poor man's oyster, this shellfish is king when it comes to our cultured products. It is said cultured mussels grown in PEI already equal or surpass those raised elsewhere to the extent that 90% of the mussels harvested in North American come from Prince Edward Island.

Should you wish to go out gathering wild mussels, look for them in rocky areas or on pilings. Do be careful not to gather from an area that is polluted such as fishing wharfs where boats may have spilled oil or parking lot runoff may make for not so clean water. They are usually in dense clusters attached by their byssal threads to rocks, muddy gravel, eel grass, wharf pilings, and other submerged objects. They can often be spotted at low tide.

**TO BUY MUSSELS**

Some local stores carry both wild and cultured mussels. Cultured mussels can be identified by their shiny black shells. Wild ones are a dull-bluish colour with barnacles and seaweed attached. The flavours are similar, but cultured mussels tend to be more tender, large meats and free of sand. The shells of fresh mussels are either closed or will close when tapped. An open shell indicates the mussel is dead and inedible.

**TO STORE MUSSELS**

* Mussels can be stored refrigerated for 2-3 days.
* Fresh mussels can be frozen in the shell by first blanching in boiling water for 20 seconds, then packing in heavy plastic bags or plastic containers.
* Cooked mussels, which have been shucked, may be frozen in plastic containers to which a 1% salt solution has been added (½ tsp sea salt per 1 cup water). Leave ½ inch headspace to allow for expansion during freezing. Mussels will keep, frozen, for 2-3 months.
* Use mussels as soon as possible.
* When using wild mussels, wash, scrape off any seaweed and barnacles, and pull off the 'beard' (whispy black hairs) sticking out of one side of the shell using a strong pocket knife. Take the beard between the knife and your thumb and pull it towards the pointed end of the shell.

Wash again. If there is a lot of sand in the pail, let the mussels soak in cold salt water to which a handful of oatmeal or cornmeal has been added. If a mussel feels heavy compared to the others, discard it. It is probably filled with mud or sand.
* cultured mussels should be rinsed just before cooking
* check that mussels are alive by tapping any open ones sharply on the counter.  If they do not close, discard.

*Antie says:*
To Cook Mussels, steam over a moderate heat for 5-10 minutes. When shells open they are cooked. In the shell, they can also be boiled, broiled, sauteed, pan fried, used in bisques, or barbecued.  Leftover mussels are excellance served in salads,  added to soups or chowers or even breaded and deeped fried.

# Oysters

The oyster has been part of the Atlantic Canadian fishery since man populated our shores. Oysters were once so cheap that there was a popular saying: 'Poverty and oysters always seem to go together.'

Wild oysters from Prince Edward Island have been harvested and exported since the 1800s. Although the first oyster farms may have been started back in Roman times, they became an important part of the Island economy in recent times.  The Malpeque oyster has become famous around the world. Many a world traveller knows PEI as the home of Anne of Green Gables and the Malpeque oyster. Not all Island oysters come from Malpeque Bay, but this is a general name used for them.  They are also marketed under other brand names.
* Oysters are found in estuaries and inlets around the coast of Atlantic Canada. The shape and quality of oysters is determined by the conditions under which they grow. On soft bottoms and crowded reefs, oysters assume a vertical position and grow long and narrow. On hard, clean, uncrowded bottoms, they grow round, strong, and deeply cupped.

Each areas unique growing conditions determine the very noticeable differences in appearance and flavour.

* Oysters in the commercial catch range from 4-6 inches.

* Oyster shells are unequal in size. The upper shell is flat and the lower shell cup-shaped. On the outside, the shells are rough and brownish or greyish-white in colour. On the inside they are smooth and dull white.

* Atlantic oysters are taken from natural beds and leased areas operated as oyster farms. Naturally-occurring oysters are harvested with tongs or rakes while cultured oysters are raised on trays or in cages. Shell strings, or other material on which oysters will attach themselves, are used for culture purposes.

* The best time for gathering oysters is at low tide. The fall is the best season of year to gather oysters. They are usually found just below the water line. Be careful when handling oysters. They are often very firmly stuck to rocks and can tear the hands. Take along a pair of work gloves.

* The oyster is known to be the only shellfish which, even if it is reared in polluted water, will cleanse itself in 24 hours if placed in clean fresh water.


**OPENING OYSTERS**

* Before opening oysters, scrub the shells clean under cold, running water. Do not let the oyster stand in water.

* To open, hold the scrubbed oyster with the cup half of the shell down. Insert a strong, blunt knife or oyster knife between the shells near the hinge or pointed end. With a twisting motion, pry the shells apart.

* When performing this operation, it is wise to hold the oyster in a folded cloth or to wear a heavy glove in case the knife slips. If you have real problems, take a hammer and chip off a spot on the outside edge. Slip the knife in and twist.

* While opening the oyster, try to retain as much of the delicious, salty juice or 'liquor' as possible.

* Once opened, slip the knife between the shells and sever the muscle holding the shells together. Sever the under muscle holding the oyster to the shell as well. Oysters are ready to serve on the half-shell or can be used in recipes.

* If they are not to be served on the half shell, drain, strain the juice through a double layer of cheesecloth to remove any particles of shell. Store oysters and juice in a tightly covered container in the refrigerator until ready to use.

**TO STORE**

* Live oysters can be stored in a damp environment within certain temperature ranges for as long as 10 weeks. When stored in the refrigerator they will remain alive for about 1 month. Shucked oysters will keep in the refrigerator for 3-4 days.

* Oysters can be successfully frozen for 4-6 months. It is not recommended that oysters be frozen in the shell. They first should be shucked and then frozen in their own juices.

*Antie says:*

*Cook only until the muscle curls around the edges.*

*DO NOT OVERCOOK - the meat will toughen and dry out. When cooking oysters in their shells, cook only until the shells open. If a shell does not open during cooking, discard the oyster, as this indicates that the oyster was not alive before cooking.*

# Crab

The most common crabs in the waters surrounding the Island are called rock crabs. These grow to an average size of 4-5 inches. Although they are very tasty, they are not a large commercial product because of their small size. They sometimes can be bought at the wharves from fishermen. Or try catching them yourself. Rock crabs can be found around bridges, wharf pilings, and in bays and inlets.

One excellent way to catch crabs is to jig for them. Simply tie a fish head to a piece of string and lower it into the water. When a crab has a really good grasp on the bait, haul it up, and catch the crab in a net or flip it onto the wharf. Catch it quickly (and carefully) before it scuttles off and back into the water. Crabs can be caught by hand in shallow water by sneaking up and grabbing them at the back of the shell. Watch out for the big front claws.

**CLEANING CRAB**

Steam or boil crab for 10-15 minutes. Cool and turn over onto its back. With a sharp knife, lift up the white apron and tear it off. Clean out lungs under the eyes. Peel off the 'devils' fingers' - the long, green, spongelike substance on each side near the topshell. Some people like to wash off the brown and green fat. Break the crab in half, crack the leg and large claws, and you are ready for eating or picking out the meat. The crabmeat is white and delicate. Don't forget to save the roe (usually yellow), as it is a great delicacy.

# Scallops

The scallop has been prized for centuries. Imagine how excited the settlers must have been when they discovered that two major scallop beds existed in the shallow waters of Northumberland Strait between Prince Edward Island and Nova Scotia.  Atlantic Canada has many rich scalloping areas. The most famous is found in southern Nova Scotia. Digby scallops are sought after around the world.

The sea scallop, also called the giant or smooth scallop, is an important commercial shellfish in Canada. The scallop has two shells, both round and almost equal in diameter, held together by a small straight hinge. The lower valve is flat, smooth and whitish in colour. The upper one is arched and usually reddish. Scallop shells are excellent for cooking in.

Normally scallops are fished with scallop draggers. They are generally not fished during the summer months. Their taste is at its best in the fall when the waters are cool.

Sea scallops prefer firm gravel, shells, or rocks to grow on. They are usually out of depth for picking unless you are scuba diving. Scallops can propel themselves through the water if disturbed. The muscle that propels the scallop is the "meat" that we eat. Scallops are normally shucked right on the boat. All but the muscle is discarded.

Scallops are becoming scarcer and fishing them more expensive. A way to farm smaller bay scallops has been discovered and is becoming more successful every year. Gone are the days when the housewife could treat scallops as an everyday dish.

**TO OPEN SCALLOPS**

Place the scallop in your left hand with the dark side of the shell down. Insert the blade of a knife in the hinge. Scoop the knife down into the far area of the bottom. Cut the muscle. Do the same on the top. Open the shell and pull the white muscle from the rest of the scallop. No further preparation is necessary. Scallops are ready for cooking. Check for any small hard pieces on the sides of the scallop and cut them away.

# Lobster

If there is anything that is symbolic of the Maritimes it must be the lobster. With modern fishing and storage methods, lobsters can be kept alive in tanks, even though they are fished in specific seasons, ensuring availability year around. Lobsters were once so plentiful and easy to catch that they were used as fertilizer for fields and gardens. Things have changed today, although the garden is still a great place to deposit your lobster shells.

The lobsters caught by commercial fishermen are trapped in wooden or wire traps which differ little in design  from those used decades ago. Lobster fishing is strictly regulated. It is illegal to catch your own.

*Antie says:*

*When listening to Maritimers talk about lobster, it becomes apparent that many prefer canners. These are smaller lobsters, normally under a pound, which are usually processed into lobster meat. The fishermen and the connoisseur will tell you this meat is more succulent than that of the larger market lobster. It's all a matter of taste.*

* The lobster that we enjoy here is the Atlantic Lobster, one of several species to be found around the world. The range of the Atlantic Lobster is from Labrador to North Carolina.
* Freshly caught lobsters are usually a dark green or mottled colour. If they are about to shed their shell, they sometimes turn a deep blue. Some lobsters are reddish, pale pink, pale blue, yellow and orange speckled, and even white. All turn red when cooked.

* Lobsters moult during the summer. They shed their hard outer shell and grow a new one. The process of shedding an old shell takes only hours, but the new shell will not harden for several months. Thus lobsters caught during the fall months may have soft shells.

* Undersized and any female lobsters who are carrying eggs are supposed to be returned to the sea. Female lobsters carry their fertilized eggs on the underside of their tails until hatched.

* Lobsters are generally between ½ pound and 4 pounds. The largest Canadian lobster ever caught weighed 37 ½ pounds.

* Live lobsters should be active, with apparent movement in the tail and claws. Be careful - those front claws can give a nasty 'bite'. That's why they are pegged or kept closed with strong elastic bands.

* Do not put them in fresh water or they will die. Generally a lobster will live up to 36 hours out of the water if kept in a cool damp environment. (Fishermen often store them in crates filled with kelp.) If live lobsters are being kept at home, keep them in the refrigerator.

**TO COOK**

* Get out your biggest pot, deep enough so lobsters will be covered.

* Islanders traditionally prefer their lobster boiled in salt water - served with no fancy trappings. For each quart of fresh water, add ¼ cup sea salt and bring to a rolling boil.

* Holding the lobster by the back with the hand or tongs, plunge it into the boiling water head first. You must have a good grip, as the lobster will be very active. Put a tight lid on the pot and return to a boil. Reduce the heat to a low boil and cook according to the weight of the lobsters.

| | |
|---|---|
| Cook a 1    lb lobster | 12 minutes |
| Cook a 1-2 lb lobster | 16 minutes |
| Cook a 2-3 lb lobster | 20 minutes |
| Cook a 3-4 lb lobster | 24 minutes |
| Cook a 5-6 lb lobster | 32 minutes |

* Lobster will turn a bright red colour when cooked. The antenna will pull off easily. This is the best test of doneness.

* Remove from the water, allow to drain and serve hot or cold.

* A 1 pound lobster yields approximately ²/₃ cup of cooked meat.

**TO FREEZE**
* Do not freeze lobster live. It must be cooked before freezing.
* Remove the meat from the shell and pack it into freezer containers.
Cover with a cold brine (2 tsp sea salt for each cup of water). Allow 2
inches headspace for expansion of the liquid. Seal securely and freeze.
Eat within 4-6 months.
* If you are going to freeze a whole lobster, place it in a plastic freez-
er bag, remove the air and seal. Or you can fill the bag with brine and
seal.


**EATING LOBSTER**
Our introduction to Maritime lobster feasts was quite an eye opener:
newspaper spread several layers thick all over the table, a chopping
block in the middle with a sturdy, sharp knife, and the only 'refinement'
- a roll of paper towels. Lobsters were cooked, dumped on the table and
we all tucked in. You either learned how to do it with the minimum of
tools or you didn't eat - at least not much.

The choice of tools you use to eat lobster is totally up to you. You can
buy picks and crackers, use nut crackers and a knife. I even have a set
with a mini hammer. True Maritime lobster lovers of the old school use
what they have on hand.

The only tools I use now are an old cleaver and a fork to slip meat out
of some of the hard-to-crack spots. Using the thumb from the smaller
claw also works for 'digging.' The only part of the lobster that sometimes defeats me is the knuckle, but inserting a spoon or fork handle
and twisting the knuckles at the joint separates them easily. Inserting
the handle end of a small spoon or fork makes it easy to scoop the suc-
cuelent knuckle meat out.

The front claws are first to go. I twist them off. I eat the knuckles and
save the succulent claws for last. Next I grab the body in one hand and
tail in the other and break the tail off sideways. The tail is opened by
holding it in one hand and squeezing so that it breaks down the middle.
I pull the shell apart and remove the meat. The dark vein in the tail
should be removed using a fork or thumb nail.

The tail fins contain very little meat. The legs are easy, break them off the body and suck the meat out. Pull the top shell off and pick out the very tender meat from the body where the legs were joined to it.

Back to my treasure. The claws are broken apart by pulling the small thumb back from the big part of the claw removing the attached car-tiledge at the same time. If you don't remove the cartiledge it will prove difficult to get the most succulent part of the lobster out of the shell without tearing. The meat will usually slide out of the small thumb with no trouble, and you can use the little hook on the end of the thumb or a fork to ease the meat out of the large claw and knuckles.

Use an old knife to crack the claw. A knife is best as it makes enough of a split to easily break the shell open. Use a chopping board - don't hold it in your hand! Meat can easily be removed from the knuckles using the handle end of a fork or spoon to twist the knuckles apart then scoop out the tasty morsel of meat. Then I turn to the next lobster.

*Antie says:*

*An easy way to serve lobster in the shell is to split the cooked lobster in half. To do this place the lobster on its back on a cutting board, using a sharp knife, split the lob-ster lengthwise from the tail by cutting through the shell and meat. Remove the dark vein in the tail. Discard the small sac or 'Lady' behind the head. The green liver or 'tomalley' and red roe are delicacies which may be eaten.*

# Snails

Snails, or escargots, are found just about everywhere there is water. The most common to our waters is the periwinkle. If someone had asked me years ago if these little black fellows were edible I would have said no, but I have since been proven wrong.

One summer while out for a walk along the shore, I noticed a couple throwing away what looked like pebbles. As I passed them, I realized they were collecting periwinkles. They were using a little metal hook (similar to a very fine crochet hook) to pop out the meat, which they ate, and then they tossed away the shells. This certainly proved to me that we do have edible snails.



*To Cook boil or steam live snails in their shells.*

* *Don't forget to wash your snails well if you get them from the beach. They can be sandy.*

* *Steam or boil for a few minutes. The snail is cooked when the brownish plate covering the entrance to the shell is loose.*

* *To eat them, take off the plate and use a pin or knife point to coax them out of the spiral shell. Go slowly for the body of the snail past the muscled foot is very delicate and can easily break off.*

All the snails found in local waters are edible but not always desirable. The major kinds are the periwinkle, the moon snail, and the whelk. Periwinkles are purple or deep blue in colour, with a 'round' shell. Periwinkles are very popular in Europe, but are not often eaten here, probably because of their small size. They taste delicious, however, despite the size. This snail can be found at low tide, clinging to sea-weed, mussel beds, wharves, pilings, or anywhere they can get a foothold.

Moon snails are covered with a brownish skin when alive, but lose this skin and turn white when washed up on the shore. They grow up to 3-4 inches in size, and can be found just beyond the low tide mark or sometimes buried in the sand. They can be recognized under water by their large, pale-blue 'foot' that spreads out about them as they move along the sea bottom. These may be safe to eat but they are so tough, it is really only feasible if you mince them for chowder or something.

Whelks are found in some areas and are a pest to fishermen when they get into the lobster traps. Small whelks can be found close to shore, but those large enough to eat are found only in deep waters. Attempts have been made to harvest whelks commercially, but this has not yet been successful. The best way to get them is to approach a lobster fishermen to see if he will save some for you.

Whelks have long pointed shells. They are sometimes called 'oyster drills.' If you pick up an empty shell on the beach that has a perfectly round hole in its side, this could have been made by the whelk in preparation for a 'meal' of fresh shellfish. Snails are not usually sold in stores. But this is not a reason to neglect them. If you are going out clamming, pick up a few snails to add to your pail. Steam them along with your shellfish.

*Antie says:*

*Fish Chowder made from local ingredients is a staple in Atlantic Canadian homes. In a chowder pot brown 1 medium chopped onion and ½ cup chopped celery in butter or olive oil. Add 2 cups diced potatoes, ½ cup sliced carrots, salt and pepper to taste, and 2 cups boiling water. Cook till tender. Add a pound or so of fish cut into pieces (white fish or salmon, fresh or frozen). Simmer about 10 minutes. Add 2 cups hot milk & heat without boiling. Serve with tea biscuits or rolls to soak up the juices.*

|  Helpful  Conversions  |  |
| --- | --- |
| 1 inch = 2.5 cm | 1 lb    = 453 g |
|  | 1/2 lb  = 225 g |
|  |  |
| 325 F  = 160 C | 1 tsp    = 5 mL |
| 350 F  = 175 C | 1 tbsp   = 15 mL |
| 375 F  = 190 C |  |
| 400 F  = 200 C | 1    cup = 250 mL |
| 450 F  = 230 C | 1/2 cup = 125 mL |
| 550 F  = 290 C | 1/3 cup =  75 mL |
|  | 1/4 cup =  50 mL |

*Antie says:*

Now that you have all of this knowledge at hand, we do urge you to get creative with seafood. Not only is it delicious and easy to prepare, it is good for you as well. Try your favourite recipes or go seeking new ones.

You can even check out other cookbooks from Seacroft. They are listed at the back of this book or on our website www.seacroftpei.com. Our cookbooks contain regional favourites as well as many contributed by well known cooks and chefs across the country.

Whether you are trying a new sandwich, or preparing a gourmet meal for family and friends, seafood will provide some new culinary experiences and cement your reputation as a fine cook.

Our wish for you is to enjoy preparing food as much as eating it, to stay health and happy, and to find great satisfaction in life.

# BOOK STORE

Seacroft, is a small publishing house located in Prince Edward Island. We produce a variety of books on several topics: folklore/history, cooking, small business/entrepreneurship, travel, and more.  Seacroft even has a line of greeting cards and calendars.  Check it all out at

www.seacroftpei.com

There will soon be some new
"Auntie Seagull...." books as well!!
and she delivers!

To order books from Seacroft check out the list on the next page and for even more topics visit our website at www.seacroftpei.com

To order now send your cheque and full mailing information (name, mailing address, phone number or email) to:
Seacroft
P.O. Box 1204
Charlottetown, PE Canada
C1A 7M8
*Want a personalized autograph, just tell us details*

# COOKBOOKS

**Seafood Cookery of Prince Edward Island**
$19.95 + $1.00 gst + $5.00 shipping = $25.95

**Seafood Menus for the Microwave
- Full Course Meals in a Flash**
$16.00 + $.80 + $4.00 shipping = $20.80

**Simple Pleasures From Our Maritime Kitchens**
(winner of the Canadian Food Culture Award from Cuisine Canada)
$20.00 + $1.00 gst + $5.00 shipping= $26.00

**Cultured Mussel Cookbook - Pioneering an Industry**
Retail Price - $13.95 + $.70 gst + $4.00 shipping = $18.65

**Sensational Seafood**
$14.95 + $.75 gst + $4.00 shipping = $18.70

**Seafood Basics......buying . storing
. cleaning . cooking fish and shellfish**
$9.95 + .50 gst + $3.50 shipping = $13.95

**Potato Basics......a potpourri of recipes, how to
and spud lore from Prince Edward Island**
$9.95 + .50 gst + $3.50 shipping = $13.95

*For more information about book content, sizes, number of pages etc.
go to www.seacroftpei.com*

www.ingramcontent.com/pod-product-compliance
Lightning Source LLC
Chambersburg PA
CBHW071524030726
47593CB00003B/1390